I0116618

# Reaching Their Potential

## Ten Important Child Development Concepts

Danielle D. Talford, M.Ed

**Reaching Their Potential: Ten Important Child Development Concepts**

Copyright © 2013 by Danielle D. Talford
DTalford Training Solutions Publication

ISBN 978-0-61580-085-1

Printed in the United States of America

All rights reserved. No part of this book may be reproduced or transmitted in any form or by any means electronic, or mechanical, including photocopying, recording, or by any information storage and retrieval system, without permission in writing from the publisher, except in the case of brief quotations embodied in critical articles and reviews. No abridgement or changes to the text are authorized by the author.

To schedule training courses, professional development workshops, speaking engagements, or for additional information visit:
www.dtalfordtrainingsolutions.org

# About the Author

**Danielle D. Talford, M.Ed,** earned a Bachelor of Science in Human Development and Family Studies with a concentration in the Lifespan from birth to death from The Pennsylvania State University. She also holds a Master of Education with a concentration in Education Management from Strayer University. Danielle spent several years as an Early Childhood Educator and Administrator and she holds Lead Teacher Certification and Level III Administrator Certification from the North Carolina Division of Child Development and Early Education.

Currently, Danielle works for the local government as an Early Intervention Service Coordinator and Infant-Toddler and Family Specialist, a certification she holds from the North Carolina Department of Health and Human Services and North Carolina Public Health. In this role, she educates caregivers (parents, grandparents, guardians, nannies, babysitters, early childhood educators) on child development and strategies to help young children with special needs maximize their developmental potential at home, in the community and in their early childhood classrooms. In addition to early intervention, Danielle is certified as a level twelve Adult Educator, which is endorsed by the North Carolina Institute for Child Development Professionals on the Early Childhood Scale and School Age Scale. This designation certifies, that she is a Masters Level Educator with at least eighteen credit hours in the areas specified.

As owner of DTalford Training Solutions, Danielle provides in-service training to Early Childhood Educators, Early Childhood Administrators, School-Age Group Leaders, and parents of young children. Danielle currently resides in Charlotte, North Carolina. There she enjoys spending time with her devoted husband Tyrome and their three beautiful boys Quentin (8), Trentin (6) and Prestin (5).

# Acknowledgements

I would like to thank God and my Lord and Savior Jesus Christ who blessed me with the knowledge and ability to write this book.

I would like to thank my wonderful and supportive husband Tyrome Talford who has been with me through thick and thin for almost 9 years. He is the person who gets me thinking and keeps me grounded.

Thank you to my children, Quentin, Trentin and Prestin, who are the inspiration for me wanting to better the lives of young children everywhere.

I am grateful for my in-laws, Linda Talford and Tenessa Moore who have always helped me with anything I need, from childcare to technical support for my company.

I would like to thank my sister Cecily Rueger who has always provided me with insight and advice.

I would like to thank my sister Adrianne Raphael for helping me with childcare and giving me support.

Thank you to my parents Marva and William Darden who worked so hard to send me to college.

Finally, I would like to express my appreciation for my dear friend and co-worker Swandolyn Lewis for always challenging me to try something new and different and for giving me support and advice.

# Forethought

Working with and raising children has definitely been a challenge. After almost a decade in the field, and as a mom, there is still a lot to learn. With children, you can never really learn all there is to know about helping them reach their developmental potential. The best any of us can do is simply soak up as much knowledge as possible, and implement it into their daily lives in order to help them learn and develop. The following words of wisdom come from my own experiences, as well as research from coursework at The Pennsylvania State University and Strayer University. My hope is that the caregivers who are parenting and educating young children, will be able to use these important ideas to help the children in their lives reach their developmental potential.

## 1. Development is a Journey

"Sometimes, reaching out and taking someone's hand is the beginning of a journey. At other times, it is allowing another to take yours."

The Perpetual Calendar of Inspiration
Vera Nazarian

# Development is a Journey

From the time of conception, the moment that the egg and sperm meet, the fetus begins its journey to becoming a fully developed baby. In utero, the heart begins to beat, limbs begin to form, and organs begin functioning; nine months later we see the first appearance. It is that glorious moment, when the baby is born, that the next adventure begins. During that journey, many people influence the path the child will take. Families and educators walk through this developmental journey together. During a child's life they develop in each of four main areas: physical (gross motor, fine motor, self-help/adaptive, receptive and expressive communication), cognitive (thinking and problem-solving), social (interaction with others), and emotional (reaction to people and situations). It is the caregiver's and educator's duty to accompany children through this journey. At times, families will do this on their own, at other times educators will be the main guide. In the end, both have an impact on the child's developmental journey. We must be willing to take the child's hand and lead them on this road, and at other times, be willing to let them take our hand and show us the path on which they need to go.

# Notes

## 2. Values and Beliefs are a Priority

"Parents are usually adjusting each value according to the particular goal they are trying to achieve for their children."

Culture and Parenting: A Guide for Delivering Parenting Curriculums to Diverse Families
Lenna L. Ontai
Ann M. Mastergeorge
Families with Young Children Workgroup

# Values and Beliefs are a Priority

There are so many theories about what is the best practice for child rearing and early childhood education. It is important to remember that not all "theories of best practice" are relevant for every child. Not only do caregivers need to respect children's unique abilities, they also need to respect the values and beliefs that come from each child's family no matter how "unusual" they seem. Of course, if something is dangerous, or threatens bodily or psychological harm to a child, it is best to forgo that cultural tradition. All caregivers need to remember, there is not one perfect way to help children develop. Educators working with young children must acknowledge the priorities and beliefs that come from individual families' values and culture.

At the same time, it is important for families to recognize that educational settings have core values and missions of their own as well. There will always be parts of our culture and belief system that may or may not make sense for the time that we live in. Use your best judgment as you incorporate values and belief systems into your approach for child rearing and early education. Also, remember that, what is best practice today could be considered absurd next year, or even next month. Instead of following any one trend, focus on your own values and beliefs as a priority.

# Notes

# 3. Let Children Be Children

"One key to avoiding many problems that accompany parenting today is to have an understanding of children's development. If we can understand the nature of the young child as it unfolds, we will be able to meet the child's real needs for balanced development of mind, body, and emotions."

You Are Your Child's First Teacher: Encouraging Your Child's Natural Development From Birth To Age Six
Rahima Baldwin Dancy

# Let Children Be Children

Even though children grow and develop quickly, caregivers need to remember that they are not little adults. Children need time and opportunities to grow and develop. They need opportunities to learn, so they can grow up and become well-adjusted, functioning adults. Think about your life. You did not get to where you are all at once, you started out as a child and developed into the self-sufficient adult that you are. Give children a chance to be children; there is plenty of time for them to learn what they need. Do not let the fast-paced society we live in fool you into thinking that you have to rush children and push them past what is reasonable. At the same time, do not put yourself in a situation in which you are so "hands-off" that the child does not reach their developmental milestones in a reasonable amount of time. This applies even if your child has additional needs that may require intervention. Remember, children need balance, so do not overdo it. No matter what the situation, always give children plenty of time and opportunity to act their age. There will be plenty of time to be an adult.

# Notes

## 4. Play is Learning

"We often forget that play is one of the most *natural* ways for human beings to learn."

From Play to Practice: Connecting Educators' Play to Children's Learning
Marcia L. Nell and Walter F. Drew, With Deborah E. Bush

# Play is Learning

Do children need to sit and look at flash cards and go through rote memorization to learn new skills? No. To learn naturally, they need to play, that *is* their work. They need to have opportunities to engage in play as much as they can within the first five years of life. Even when they begin formal education, children benefit from their experiences during play. Though many caregivers would like it to be so, play does not always have to be organized; sometimes it can be chaotic. That is perfectly alright, as children need opportunities to express themselves so that they can become thinkers. Play gives them unique opportunities to develop life and learning skills. Remember, the goal is to provide a balance. In order to do that, play should consist of both adult-directed and child-directed activities. Ideas for indoor and outdoor play include: dramatic and sensory play as well as fine motor/manipulative object play. Other activities include: art, nature/science, writing, reading, blocks, math/counting and music/movement. Give children the opportunity to play with adults, with each other, independently, and in a variety of areas as much as possible each day so that they can continue to learn and develop.

# Notes

## 5. Pay Attention to Children's Interests

"Knowing children well is key to providing learning experiences that are most appropriate for them."

Learning at Home PreK-3: Homework Activities That Engage Children and Families
Ann C. Barbour

# Pay Attention to Children's Interests

As adults, we typically have an agenda when it comes to children. Parents may want to teach their child a certain skill, so we buy a specific toy or try to engage children in a particular activity to help the child learn that skill. Educators write lesson plans that reflect the theme of the week or suggestions for activities based on the curriculum. The issue is that what we like or expect may not be what interests the child. We must pay attention to what motivates them and stimulates their curiosity. They should have a say in what they are, or are not, interested in doing. Now, some children may have narrow interests, and we will want to help them explore broader learning opportunities. This is perfectly acceptable, but we need to remember to give them plenty of opportunities to do things that they are interested in, as well. So, pay attention to what gets the attention of the children you educate and care for, and expand on their development and learning opportunities using the materials and activities they already enjoy, while incorporating some new things they may not have yet discovered.

# Notes

## 6. Use a Variety of Materials

"Young children are explorers and it is the job of the adults around them to provide materials to stimulate their development."

Jean Piaget

# Use a Variety of Materials

It is natural for parents and educators to jump on the bandwagon of the hottest new toy or activity. As society changes, toys and activities will adjust and evolve. Some toys will be great for stimulating development, while others may not. The most important thing to remember is that children need a variety of materials with which they can play and interact. Materials should consist of some store-bought items and many homemade items, made out of recycled materials that are safe for children. When purchasing toys, always check the age recommendations before allowing children to play with them. When making items, protect young children; by ensuring there are no pieces that can break off and potentially become a choking hazard or cause injury. Also, clean the toys thoroughly and let them air-dry to avoid other forms of contamination. Always provide children opportunities to play and interact with a variety of toys, safe materials, and an environment that stimulates their development.

# Notes

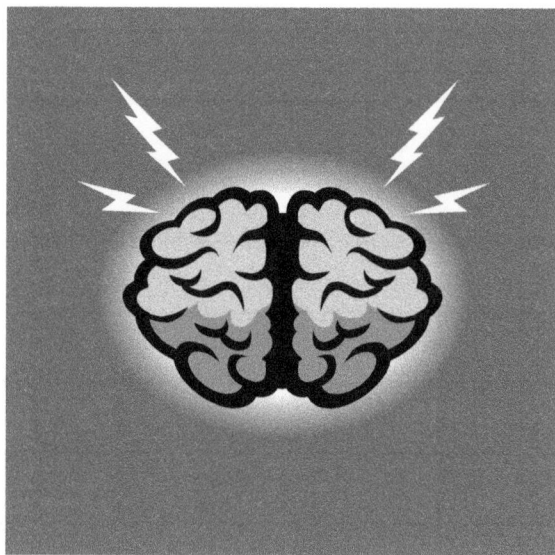

## 7. Help Children Exercise Their Memory

"The act of remembering comes naturally for most people. But memory is like so many functions of the brain: the more we exercise it, the stronger it becomes."

The Whole-Brain Child: 12 Revolutionary Strategies to Nurture Your Child's Developing Mind
Daniel J. Siegel, M.D
Tina Payne Bryson, Ph.D.

# Help Children Exercise Their Memory

Again, we are not talking about flash cards and rote memorization. There are two hemispheres in the brain. We use the left hemisphere for logic and facts. The right hemisphere is for creativity and imagination. To help children reach their maximum potential it is best to strengthen both hemispheres. You can help children exercise the right side of their brain by having them create works of art, music, dances, or plays and skits. Then you can help them exercise the left side of their brain by asking them to recall facts and details about their day. For example, exercise the child's right brain, by having them create a picture with different materials. Then, exercise their left brain by asking the child questions about a picture they made. Ask details about why they made the picture, who they made it for, and other details about it. Take notes, so you can remember their responses. That evening, or the next day, have the child look at the picture again and ask the same questions. If the child has forgotten, remind them of the details they gave you before. Try this again a few days later to see how much they have retained. Help children exercise their mind and memory by giving them opportunities to create and then engaging them in conversations about their creations and other daily activities.

# Notes

# 8. Know the Child's Individual or Special Needs

"For children with disabilities, we know that in order to design intervention that is effective, we must have a clear grasp of the child's current developmental skills."

Working with Families of Young Children With Special Needs
Edited by Robin A. McWilliam, PhD
Series Editors' Note by Karen R. Harris and Steve Graham

# Know the Child's Individual or Special Needs

There are so many people who are in denial about their child's individual or special needs. There are so many disabilities that affect learning and development Autism Spectrum Disorder, Mental Retardation Spectrum Disorder, Attention Deficit Disorder, and Attention Deficit-Hyperactivity Disorder, just to name a few. People are so fearful of "labels" that they live in denial.

Let's get one thing out in the open, ALL people are labeled. No matter what you do to shelter your child, one day, someone, somewhere is going to put a label on him or her whether they are very different or just slightly different from their peers. Even children who develop fairly appropriately can end up with a "label." Parents need to stop worrying about what someone is going to say about their child if they are diagnosed with a special need, and instead focus on the child's future. The purpose of this book is for caregivers to help young children reach their developmental potential. If parents are blinded by fear of what the educators will say about their child, and educators are fearful to say anything to parents because they do not want to upset them, the only one who will suffer is the child. All children are special, but not all children have special needs that require extra attention. If you suspect something is wrong, speak up until your concerns are heard. For children zero to age three contact the Early Intervention Branch in your area for children three and older contact the Public and Local Education Agency. Parents can also try contacting the child's pediatrician or primary care physician; they can assist you in getting the child evaluated. If a child does not appear to be developing quite like their peers, caregivers should not hesitate to seek advice immediately and educators should not hesitate to refer families to specialists, so that any current individual or special needs do not hinder the child's future development.

# Notes

## 9. Communication is a Vital Tool

"When you take the time to actually listen, with humility, to what people have to say, it's amazing what you can learn. Especially if the people who are doing the talking also happen to be children."

Stones Into Schools: Promoting Peace With Books, Not Bombs, in Afghanistan and Pakistan
Greg Mortenson

# Communication is a Vital Tool

Caregivers are spending less and less time talking to children. This happens in homes and in early education facilities. Televisions, computers, and other technology devices will never compare to good old-fashioned face-to-face conversation. When communicating directly with children, they have the opportunity to learn appropriate social-emotional and communication skills. From infancy, when caregivers respond to a babies cry in a timely and positive manner, it teaches them that the world is a safe place and that someone cares enough about them to meet their needs. As a child develops, they learn that they can use words and gestures to communicate how they feel and what they want, as well as understand what others feel or expect from them. Each day, we should engage children by talking to them. In infancy, we may talk to a baby as they coo back at us. As the child ages, we communicate with them by asking questions and allowing them to ask us questions. There should always be a balance between caregivers talking to children and listening to children. Use communication as a tool, talk to children so they will learn how to talk to you.

# Notes

# 10. Relationships are Essential to Children's Success

"Parent engagement is an overarching principle and approach for involving families in decisions about themselves, their children, services, and their communities."

Growing and Sustaining Parent Engagement: A Toolkit for Parents and Community Partners
Center for the Study of Social Policy

# Relationships are Essential to Children's Success

Parents and educators should always be working together to help children reach their developmental potential. Without a strong parent-educator team, the child will have a difficult time finding success in school and in life. Both parent and educator need to be willing to communicate and compromise, giving a little and taking a little, in order to reach their common goal. Parents must remember that their child is one of many in a classroom, and that the educator must balance the needs of one child with that of the group. Educators need to appreciate that some children and families require more attention and maintenance than others, and they should be willing to give them the necessary support for the family to feel satisfied with the quality of care and education their child is receiving. Parents and educators must make a concerted effort to develop a good relationship, with reasonable expectations of each other, in order for children to truly succeed.

# Notes

# Summary

To help young children reach their developmental potential there are ten important concepts caregivers need to understand. (1) We must think of a child's development as a journey; sometimes adults take the lead, at other times the child is the leader. (2) Caregivers need to know that values and beliefs are a priority, even if they are not the trend at any given time. (3) Adults must remember to let children be children and not try to make them little adults. (4) An important concept to remember is that play is learning for young children. (5) We need to pay attention to a child's interests so that they enjoy learning. (6) Remember to use a variety of age appropriate materials, both store-bought and homemade to enhance the learning experience. (7) Caregivers should help children exercise their memory by engaging both the creative side and the logical side to enhance overall brain development. (8) Parents and educators must be honest and aware of the child's individual or special needs and avoid being in denial or focusing on labels. (9) No matter what direction society goes in, caregivers must remember that communication is vital, and they must not let too much technology in at the cost of face-to-face contact with children. (10) Finally, relationships between parents and educators are essential to success; compromising with and understanding the other party are essential to establishing a beneficial relationship.